LEFT BEHIND

THE ABANDONED HISTORY OF NORTHERN CALIFORNIA AND THE SAN FRANCISCO BAY AREA

MANOL Z. MANOLOV

AMERICA THROUGH TIME®
ADDING COLOR TO AMERICAN HISTORY

This book is dedicated to my guru, Paramhansa Yogananda,
and to my family, with the deepest gratitude and love.

America Through Time is an imprint of Fonthill Media LLC
www.through-time.com
office@through-time.com

Published by Arcadia Publishing by arrangement with Fonthill Media LLC
For all general information, please contact Arcadia Publishing:
Telephone: 843-853-2070
Fax: 843-853-0044
E-mail: sales@arcadiapublishing.com
For customer service and orders:
Toll-Free 1-888-313-2665

www.arcadiapublishing.com

First published 2020

ISBN 978-1-63499-219-0

Typeset in Trade Gothic 10pt on 15pt
Printed and bound in England

CONTENTS

ACKNOWLEDGMENTS

A BIG THANK YOU goes out to Anna-Kaisa for her endless patience, support and the many hours spent editing—I couldn't have done it without you! Also, a thank you to Stefan for his editing work and for keeping me honest. I'm very grateful to Jon Haeber for providing information about the enigma that has been the Richmond General Warehouse and, of course, to the Port of Richmond for allowing me to spend time inside that fascinating building.

AUTHOR'S NOTE

THE AIM OF THIS BOOK is to present a variety of abandoned historic sites in the Northern California Bay Area, in their current state, through images and words. I will also share a bit of background information about each place, but will do so in a brief manner, for this is not intended to be a comprehensive history. Rather, it is an introduction to the region's abandoned legacy that hopefully allows the reader to form their own impressions and opinions. Ultimately, I consider this more of a photographic work than one of pure writing, and it is my hope that the images will be able to mostly speak for themselves.

INTRODUCTION

VERILY, WE LIVE IN A WORLD AFRAID OF DEATH.

As an explorer of abandoned places, I often ponder upon this thought while wandering through yet another destination where few others ever venture. If anyone is even aware of their existence in the first place, the decaying and ruined historical sites I spend my time in are usually shunned, discarded and confined to the shadows—out of sight, out of mind. Perhaps, because most of us do not appreciate the uncomfortable reminders that everything on this Earth, including humans, has an expiration date, we choose to ignore the fleeting aspect of life as much as possible.

But if death indeed gives meaning to life, then the monuments of history that now exist in decay and desolation are not to be avoided but rather investigated for what they can teach us about ourselves. Despite the fact that these sites might be our reminder about where we've come from and where we're eventually headed, if we can somehow surmount our initial dislike for their outward appearance, we might find plenty there to value and learn from.

For myself, I've never seen these abandoned sites in any sort of negative light. In fact, quite the opposite—to me they are pockets of quiet solitude and they emit a sense of peace that I can't seem to find in the noisy, crowded, modern society that most everyone else prefers to exist in. Contrary to their outward appearance, they still vibrate with the energy of a different, simpler time, and feel very much alive. To me, these visits have always been a peculiar but very much effective distraction from the confines and demands of the modern, stressful world. It's one of the best forms of therapy I know.

Aside from personal sentiment, however, there is also a social importance and cultural significance to the abandoned places that live on the outskirts of our society. As they sit, quietly rotting away, our common history and heritage disappears with them. And as it often is the case in the Bay Area, apartment buildings and tech complexes grow up in their place.

My initial fascination with the deserted parts of my region was of a purely visual and photographic nature. It didn't take long, however, before I began making a conscious attempt to document as much of their vanishing world as possible, because regardless of how they are viewed, these places do have a story to tell and are important in their own way. They represent a captivating treasure trove, revealing much about the stages we have passed through as a society, while looking to find our way in the vast scheme of things. And since few seem to care about the past when the present and future hold so much material allure, it might just be up to us explorers to preserve much of this history for future generations.

So, then, why Northern California and the Bay Area? Simply because this is the place that I have lived in for a long while now, and all these fascinating sites exist right in my backyard. Yes, my backyard is filled with abandoned naval air stations and former military installations the size of small towns. The obscure and awkward are here as well, in the form of ghost towns and islands that once extended an unfriendly welcome to immigrants attempting to start a new and better life on the soil of San Francisco.

If there is any pattern in my work, it seems that most of what I've visited and continue to visit always has a tinge of military history. Aside from my personal interest, this is because Northern California has always been an area with a significant military presence, and nowadays, it is consequently an area with a significant abundance of military ghosts. Many of these sites have been sitting deserted for decades—some were the victims of the Base Realignment and Closure (BRAC) process at the end of the Cold War, while others have fallen prey to the rapid growth and tumultuous change still engulfing the Bay Area today. Though now relieved from active duty, these military monoliths are still very much emblematic of the region I am documenting in my work. After all, Jimmy Doolittle and his raiders departed for Tokyo in April 1942 aboard the USS *Hornet* from one of the piers of Naval Air Station Alameda, and Joe DiMaggio, Jimmy Hendrix and Clint Eastwood once passed through the grounds of Fort Ord for basic training.

At the time of this writing, many unintentional time capsules still dot the landscapes of the Northern California Bay Area, but as development and the twisted realities of overpopulation encroach on their space, time is swiftly running out. If one day in the future we look back and question why everything turned out the way it did in the isolated technological bubble that is the San Francisco Bay Area, I hope we can come across the realization that the consequences of neglecting our history and mismanaging the legacy that it has bequeathed upon us, are often greater and farther reaching than we might think. Because the point here is not necessarily urban exploration and the tickle of the forbidden one might feel from such activities, but rather perhaps the commentary that this abandoned history makes on the bigger human condition and on where our values and morals truly lie. For pondering such concepts enables an analytical process vitally important to making decisions that ultimately shape the world we live in.

The all-too-prevalent thinking in the haven of technological advancement that is the Bay Area of today, seems to be that the future is all that matters. That once items are no longer useful, we can abandon them, because we can quickly and cheaply create new ones. And that we can keep on living in the same unconscious way we always have, selfishly mired in overt consumerism, taking more than giving, and just create better technology to fix our blunders.

But the past is always with us, always relevant though old, and its lessons can be invaluable. Our attitude toward it, toward heritage and placing worth not only upon the new, modern and material, but also upon culture and preservation, can perhaps hold clues as to how we can adjust our attitudes and activities to create a better and less destructive human experience. Because, as the famous dictum goes, if we choose to ignore history, we are destined to repeat its errors.

Northern California
September 2019

1

NAVAL AIR STATION ALAMEDA

Standing face to face with the remains of the former Naval Air Station Alameda for the first time is an unforgettable experience. The sheer vastness of the now uninhabited open space, combined with the enormous structures rusting and decaying in plain sight, lends the place a post-apocalyptic look that makes for a most impressive view. I first drove up on the perimeter road snaking right along the edge of the water, past the ferry terminal and the Oakland harbor, in the autumn of 2011. At the end of the embankment, as I glanced over to my left, I immediately came face to face with the complex's main gate and checkpoint. There was no barrier, no guard. Abandoned though it was, I still could not believe that I could just casually walk into what used to be one of the most secure and off-limits naval bases in Northern California.

The former Naval Air Station once had many faces. Along with naval operations, aircraft maintenance facilities, personnel housing and various amenities (tennis courts, bowling alley, a six-hole golf course, Officers' Club and pool, to name a few), the compound also housed one of the Bay Area's biggest military airports. The two 8,000-ft. runways, overgrown and unused, still crisscross the western tip of the base today.

Personnel stationed here enjoyed views of the San Francisco skyline and plenty of open space inside the complex, where perfectly trimmed lawns and manicured hedges abounded. Daycare centers that catered to the needs of those living on base with children and an Officers' Wives' Club were only a few of the many morale, welfare and recreation facilities that existed on site. Throughout fifty-seven years of naval operations, Navy ships, aircraft and aircraft carriers based in NAS Alameda participated in many conflicts, including both the Korean and Vietnam wars. At the height of its sprawl in 1997, the base's area comprised one-third of the island of

Alameda. It was in that same year that the naval air station was cut down by BRAC and its doors reluctantly opened to the public for the first time.

Ever since then, soccer fields, gyms, breweries and various businesses have been sprouting up on site, spurred to growth by the ashes of the old station. To date, aside from the USS *Hornet* museum ship and a small collection of exhibits at the Alameda Naval Air Museum, almost nothing else of the place's legacy has been preserved. Conservation seems to be on no one's mind, and any thoughts of such actions are hindered, once again, by the allure of the huge chunk of prime Bay Area real estate the carcass of the Alameda Naval Air Base occupies.

One of my favorite spots to visit on the old base is a location that does not require sneaking into. It is the CV-12 aircraft carrier, the successor to the original USS *Hornet* (CV-8) that ferried the Doolittle Raiders and their B-25 Mitchell aircraft on their way to bomb Japan from the air for the first time in World War II. That first *Hornet* departed from the Alameda Naval Air Station in April 1942, and later participated in the Battle of Midway, before being sunk in the Battle of the Santa Cruz Islands in October 1942. The second manifestation of that mighty ship now resides at the southernmost pier of the former base, serving as a permanent museum. Every time I scale the steep ladder up the vessel's side and walk its enormous top deck, I am reminded that I am actually standing on a piece of history, amidst the very surroundings that shaped its unique story. I am also reminded that it is a small miracle the USS *Hornet* still exists to tell its tales, docked at the piers of Alameda, instead of living another incarnation at the hands of a scrap metal metamorphosis. The way things are going, the rest of what they now call Alameda Point might not be as lucky.

Exterior of Building 169, located close to the manmade lagoon and seaplane ramps.

Decrepit exterior of the NAS Alameda DeCA (Defense Commissary Agency) commissary. Here, military personnel and their families could buy groceries at discounted prices.

The Catholic sacristy room inside the NAS Alameda main chapel.

The mammoth hangars of the Naval Air Rework Facility (NARF) cover a staggering one million square feet, and are one of the most contaminated areas of the former Naval Air Station.

Above: An old distribution transformer next to the Naval Air Rework Facility (NARF), or Building 5, where aircraft repair and maintenance took place.

Right: An admittance telephone still attached to the outside wall of one of the naval base buildings.

Left: Entrance to the Transition Assistance building.

Below: A classroom blackboard inside one of the Transition Assistance building rooms.

A glimpse into one of the classrooms of the Transition Assistance building.

Inside one of the Navy Exchange main barracks, a decal of the HM-19 "Golden Bears," a U.S. Navy helicopter mine countermeasures squadron, still decorates a door.

A lampshade sits deserted in a closet inside one of the enlisted men's barracks. Someone once lived here.

This Mobile Rescue School truck had found its final resting spot next to a building at the southeastern tip of the base.

The woodwork of these cabinets has severely degraded since the days when the NAS Alameda gate house was in operation.

Storage cabinets inside the NAS Alameda gate house. They once held various documents and forms, such as "Permissive Authorization for Search and Seizure," as one of the shelf labels still states.

File cabinets and desks that once surely served vital functions, now sit deserted inside the gate house of NAS Alameda.

Secure-looking enclosure inside the gate house (main entry point) of NAS Alameda. A similar looking contraption on the second floor suggests the building might have also been used as some sort of temporary detaining area.

Intimidating staircase inside the former gate house.

Inside Building 5—the Naval Air Rework Facility or NARF. Residue from radium paint used in aircraft dials and other chemicals used in repairing aircraft engines has resulted in this being one of the most contaminated areas of NAS Alameda.

2

DRAWBRIDGE

D rawbridge is a unique contradiction. It is a local legend, yet one so obscure and buried in oblivion, that to this day not many people are aware of the place's existence. A shortage of publicly accessible information, a somewhat poorly documented past and a location that is literally cut off from the rest of the San Francisco Bay Area's South Bay have all contributed to the mystery of the region's only ghost town.

The trek out to Drawbridge, along the still-functioning railroad tracks, is an adventure in itself. It takes one through marshy paths, under colossal power lines and by remains of the Cargill Salt Works' now defunct operations. The salt ponds and their otherworldly landscapes still ornament the long walk and one spends almost as much time sightseeing during the journey, as at the destination. It feels like no time at all has passed when the railroad tracks come into sight, marking the final leg of the journey. And once the first buildings begin to appear from the monotonous scenery of the slough, it is hard to believe what your eyes are beholding. A small patch of an entirely different existence stands in contrast to the modern Silicon Valley, which completely surrounds the tiny settlement, and the feeling that one has been transplanted to another world is overwhelming. Wooden structures of all shapes and sizes (houses, hotels and even a gun club), half-sunken into the unstable, marshy soil, flank the railroad that still carries passengers on the Union Pacific lines.

In fact, it all began with the narrow gauge South Pacific Coast railroad (no longer in existence), when in 1876 a small cabin for the drawbridge operator became the first structure set down on the location of where the town of Drawbridge would one day stand. The heyday of the settlement came later, during the 1920s, when the town grew large enough to be divided into two neighborhoods—the Protestant north and the Roman Catholic south—remains of which are still visible today. During the

Prohibition, speakeasies and brothels abounded and even the police were reluctant to enter this out-of-the-way locale, because of its unsavory reputation for lawlessness.

It was a romantic concept in theory, but Drawbridge was doomed from the very beginning. The tiny town was built on marshland, elevated from the sea by only seven feet. When groundwater was lost to agricultural use, the soft soil underneath the structures began to slowly give way. The fish and shrimp that had long sustained its residents fell prey to water pollution as raw sewage from nearby cities and agricultural runoff from farms began to flow into the bay in the 1930s. Unregulated duck hunting depleted the bird population and all but eliminated yet another source of food for the residents.

With conditions deteriorating rapidly, people left one by one until Charles Luce and his dog were the last ones standing. They held their ground until 1979, with Luce often having to drive away looters from his premises with a shotgun. After that, the fully deserted Drawbridge was left to nature's devices, and it has been gradually disappearing into the marsh below ever since. The consensus is that the island upon which Drawbridge still lies will eventually disappear altogether as soil deteriorates and sea levels continue to rise.

It would be hard to find a more surreal place than Drawbridge in the entire Bay Area, and soon, it will be hard to find it at all. Today, very little is left of what was once a thriving town in a very unusual location, and as the remaining structures continue to slowly sink into the bay, they take with them the colorful stories and characters of another era.

Sun rays filter through the skeletons of a row of homes in northern Drawbridge.

The empty space of a Drawbridge dwelling's windowpanes provides a frame for the distant East Bay hills. In the foreground, morbidly-themed graffiti decorates the woodwork.

A cluster of twisted Drawbridge shacks adorns the lonesome Union Pacific Railroad.

The San Francisco Bay Area—old and new. A view from Drawbridge toward the town of Milpitas.

A corrugated iron shed lives out its last among the marsh. The view is from a neighboring wooden home, facing westward, toward the Pacific Ocean.

The corrugated iron roofs on some dwellings seem to have done little to prevent their decay at the hands of the elements.

A chimney outlet, water pipes and random hardware still cling to the walls of yet another sinking Drawbridge home.

The remains of what used to be the Gordon Gun Club.

Left: A wooden sink that was once part of a Drawbridge home's kitchen. The marshland visible in the lower part of the picture has now become the floor of these structures and is slowly swallowing them whole.

Below: The sun sets, both figuratively and literally, on what remains of a wooden home in the Roman Catholic (south) neighborhood of Drawbridge.

3

PIER 70

One of the biggest thrills in exploring abandoned places is the accidental find—those times when you happen to stumble upon a really magnificent site completely out of nowhere. My run-in with San Francisco's now nearly forgotten Pier 70 was a perfect example of this marvelous occurrence. A stroll down one street, a casual left on another, and all of a sudden, I was face to face with the famous Bethlehem Steel Administration Building—the impressive headquarters of the company that once ran the massive shipyard operations on the city's eastern waterfront.

Straddling the north-east corner of Illinois and 20th Street, the structure is an office building of rare beauty and refinement. Designed by Fredrick H. Meyer, a once famous San Francisco architect, and built in 1917 in the Classical Revival style, it presents an epic sight despite its now decrepit condition. It didn't take long before the appearance of Bethlehem Steel's executive building made me realize that I must be in the vicinity of the Pier 70 complex. Surely enough, a more careful glance about revealed the huge outlines of some of the iconic site's structures lurking in the background. Luckily, I had a camera with me that day.

A bit of wandering about, a few encounters with security guards of certain tech companies that now occupy some of the restored old Pier 70 buildings, and before long I was making my way into the strangely quiet compound that once housed the oldest civilian shipyard in the United States and produced the first steel ships to set out on the Pacific. It was Sunday, and though the Pier 70 grounds are currently undergoing work to clean up and "modernize" the space to include lofts, businesses and also "rehabilitate historic resources", whatever that might mean, all was quiet. It wasn't difficult to soon find myself on the inside of Plate Shop #2, also known as Building #12.

This particular building has two stories and its construction dates back to 1941. Its purpose once lay in the cutting and forming of steel plates for repairing the hulls of ships. Once inside, it was hard to perceive the energy and atmosphere of the original building. Obviously, work was being done to either dismantle the structure or to begin some level of renovation and signs of recent human presence were all around. Yellow flags were stretched out on lines across the open space, and the torn ground was marked by bright orange spray paint lines in various spots. Not very enamored with the first floor, I almost missed the stairwell, tucked away in a corner and camouflaged against the dark, rusting metal, as I was heading for the exit.

Initially, all that the elevation revealed was a bird's eye view of the first floor ceiling's tangled metal supports. Persevering further up, however, I soon came upon the entrance to the top level. Almost immediately artifacts of all sorts appeared before me—chairs, old Polaroid photographs, period piece bathroom facilities and even a scaled-down model of a submarine that was sitting in the middle of the enormous top floor. A vintage sign painted upon the wall decades ago pointed out the way to the drafting room, and an enticing-looking sky tunnel connected Building #12 to neighboring Warehouse #2. However, my hopes for further exploration were quickly dashed when I discovered the door was securely locked.

When I finally emerged from the enclosure, I once again realized the enormity of the Pier 70 landscape. I was surrounded by buildings that dated back to the original World War II-era complex, with some structures being even older. As this was quite the unexpected visit, I did not have the luxury of more time. I had to make my way back, and hope to be able to return again and document more of the once famous pier. After all, it was also here that the Union Iron Works produced materials for some of San Francisco's most iconic buildings in the nineteenth century, and it was here that a variety of local shipbuilding operations, dating as far back as the California Gold Rush, once existed. Nowadays, the plan of the powers that be is to turn this famous pier into a just right "mix of preservation and development." Given my sentiments, it is probably needless to say it, but I maintain that it will be a shame of epic proportions if this bastion of local lore is let to suffer such a fate.

The Bethlehem Steel Administration building—my first hint that I was in the vicinity of history.

Corrugated iron abounds in Building #21, the Electric Shop/Substation #5. Dating back to 1900, it is Pier 70's oldest remaining steel structure.

The chaotic yard right next to Building #21 still shows some signs of human presence.

The Convoy Company once used to operate on the premises.

The decrepit first floor of the Plate Shop #2 building shows signs of recent construction work that will likely usher it into an uncertain future.

I passed this vibrantly colored gate on my way to the higher floors of what's known as Building #12.

Ruined bathroom facilities on the top floor of the Plate Shop #2 building.

I came across these Polaroids depicting a variety of old cars. Handwriting on one of the pictures showed the date 3/23/1999.

View toward the docks from Building #12—Plate Shop #2. Building #21, the Electric Shop/Substation #5 and the Noonan Building are visible on the left.

A vintage graphic on one of the Building #12 walls points out the way to the drafting room.

Another one of the bathroom facilities in Building #12 presents a sorry sight.

The concrete sky-tunnel connecting Building #12 to the neighboring Warehouse #2. Unfortunately, the door was locked.

The topmost floor of Plate Shop #2 presents vast vistas of decades of industrial decay.

A model of what looks to be a submarine is the lone occupant of Plate Shop #2's second floor.

4

FORT ORD

Fort Ord is in many ways the quintessential California abandonment—a colossal ex-army post, located amidst picturesque surroundings, just minutes away from the Pacific Ocean's postcard shores. For its sheer enormity and variety of content, it might well have been called the City of Fort Ord. It is because of these reasons also that Fort Ord is one of the most fascinating abandoned sites in Northern (or perhaps Central, in this case) California. Its vast area and diverse history makes seeing all it has to offer in a single visit impossible. Because of its complexity, my personal fascination with the place and the nine years of visits I've embarked on so far, Fort Ord can justly be regarded as the centerpiece of this book. They way I've chosen to present this leviathan is by dividing the base into sections, and presenting different areas of it through the pictures below this text.

Now another victim of the BRAC process, the vast camp came into being as an artillery range in 1917, and after many name changes, it derived its last and current moniker from Union Army Major General Edward Otho Cresap Ord. In 1941, expanded in size and use, the area became formally designated as a fort. It saw active use during World War II and the Korea and Vietnam Wars as a basic training center and troop staging area. The complex functioned on an enormous scale, spanning almost forty-four square miles and housing over 50,000 personnel during the height of World War II. Throughout the years of its existence, Fort Ord had its own police and fire departments, an Olympic-size swimming pool, sauna, bowling alley, an eighteen-hole golf course, tennis courts and a variety of sports fields. It also featured eleven chapels, employing a total of twenty-three chaplains, a preschool, multiple elementary schools and a junior high school.

I first spotted the grand remains of Fort Ord entirely by accident. Sometime in 2010, I was driving north on Highway 1 on the way back from Monterey, when out of the corner of my eye I caught a few details that had previously escaped my notice. The jagged lines, peeling paint and faded colors barely peering out from behind the dense foliage were those of the old World War II-era barracks which, at the time of this writing, still decorate the grounds of the fort. Fascinated by the strange sight, I returned soon after for what would be the first of many trips to this exposed sarcophagus of military history.

During those first visits in 2010 and 2011, I encountered a plethora of artifacts and buildings that are no longer there today. Many structures (such as the entire Engineering Compound Facility) have since been torn down to make room for development of the lucrative real estate space that has either already taken place, or is coming in the near future. The signs of human presence once found lying about these now demolished buildings (computers, telephones, documents, furniture) have correspondingly been reduced to ashes, as well. Throughout the years, as the ceaseless development around it encroaches on its premises, less and less of Fort Ord remains standing.

In 1994, Fort Ord was the largest U.S. military base to close its doors when BRAC came calling. Jimi Hendrix, Clint Eastwood and Jerry Garcia once passed through its grounds for basic training. But now, on the eve of yet more change, what remains of the historic base is slowly giving way to an uncertain future. A future where the jagged lines, twisted boards and fading colors of another era will most likely be dead and gone forever.

ENGINEERING COMPOUND FACILITY

A seat with a view near one of the Engineering Compound Facility buildings.

A glovebox lays discarded on the ground near the Engineering Compound Facility.

The inside of this Engineering Compound Facility building is filled with documents, old computers, desks and chairs. Most of these structures date back to the World War II era and are severely dilapidated.

Once the holder of important documents, this binder now sits forgotten and covered in asbestos dust.

Office furniture has now become fodder for vandals and the elements.

A place of rest amidst the ruins.

WORLD WAR II BARRACKS

Seemingly endless rows of derelict barracks buildings are now being engulfed by the surrounding vegetation.

A discarded memento from New Year's Day 1992.

Above left: File cabinets in one of the World War II-era administration buildings.

Above right: With no better use for it, a telephone receiver protrudes from the broken window of a World War II-era barracks structure, having been thrown right through by an unknown force.

Below: A telephone left behind in one of the barracks administration buildings still has the names of its assigned contacts attached to it.

User manual for the dBase database management system.

Toilet closet inside one of the wooden barracks buildings. The pamphlets scattered about contain information about the Army career and alumni program.

Bathroom facilities on the first floor of a World War II-era barracks.

Spicy wallpaper inside the kitchen of what looked to be a sort of recreation and leisure facility, that also featured a full, wood-trimmed bar.

Chapels

An original Allen organ sits disemboweled inside the chapel it once served.

Broken pews line the interior of this Fort Ord chapel, which has remarkably retained some of its original features, despite being vandalized.

The model T-44 organ was manufactured by the Allen Organ Company.

Inside a Fort Ord chapel that has seen better days. Almost nothing is left of the original structure's furnishings and artifacts.

The exterior of a Ford Ord chapel, now enveloped in creepers.

MODERN BARRACKS

Left: The U.S. Army 9th Infantry Regiment, nicknamed the "Manchus," was housed in this building. They decorated one of its entrances accordingly. Sharpshooter badges, paratrooper jump wings and Ranger insignia complete the design.

Below: Wall decal in one of the modern barrack buildings. The Manchus is a reference to the nickname of 9th Infantry Regiment of the United States Army. The regiment was based out of Fort Ord in the late 1980s.

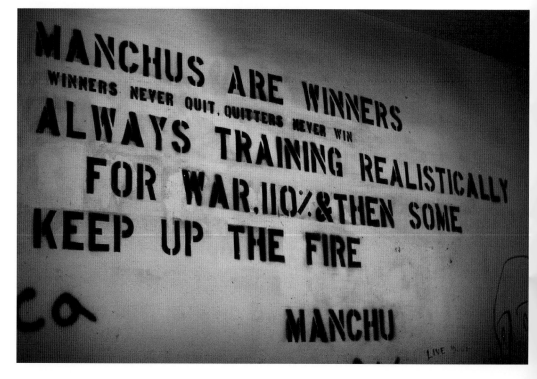

What's left of a kitchen facility on the first floor of a modern barracks building.

Vintage ad for Carlton cigarettes inside a modern barracks room.

A classic Budweiser beer can in one of the bathroom facilities.

An old "Army—Be All You Can Be" decal is partially hidden beneath a camouflaged wall.

Mattresses and furniture still populate the rooms where soldiers once lived.

Nasty Boys soldier art in the basement of a modern barracks building.

The soldiers housed in the modern barracks were very creative in embellishing their living quarters with artful representations of their various companies and units. Here, we are about to enter the Mortar Pit.

Bathroom facility inside one of the modern barracks buildings.

Sniper decal soldier art still ornaments a barracks wall.

I don't think anyone would ever doubt the ruggedness of the 14th Combat Engineer Battalion. And their artist skills are no less impressive.

A wall decal motto emblazoned upon the American flag.

Sharpie soldier art depicting paratroopers in action.

3rd Platoon "Nasty Boys" soldier art on an inside barrack wall.

...RLY, A	*VANMETER, B	*MUELLER, M
TES, M	*PHILLEY, B	KEZESKE, S
...ES, E	*HEDRICK, D	*CHARGOIS, ...
...FT, E	*LEE, F	JACKSON, C
SON, M	*TRACY, M	MONTGOMER...
...KCLIFF, W	*FRANKLIN, M	HAMILTON, ...
...NLEY, T	GULLATT, D	MCKINNEY, C
...SSON, M	ALLRED, F	KNOUSE, L
...TH, M	*HOGELIN, C	*WYNNE, T
...BLEDO, E	BIGGS, Z	HJORT, D
...LALOBOS, J	BURNS, J	MIZE, A
...SIER, J	GAGNIER, D	WOLFE, P
...NTIAGO, E	OLSEM, S	MEYER, M

A roster of the "Nasty Boys" of 3rd Platoon.

This football table belonged to the U.S. Army 14th Engineer Battalion. Seen in a recreation room inside one of the modern barracks.

Paint Shop

These Harco printing presses appeared in excellent condition and it seemed to me that they would start back up instantly if only someone was around to plug them in.

Chairs lie in a pile inside one of the paint shop rooms. Some looked new and still had plastic foil wrapped around them.

Storage room with stern warning sign inside the paint shop.

MOTOR POOL AREA

"Where computers go to die"—a scene near the motor pool compound.

A vehicle ramp near the motor pool area is subtly accented by a discarded fire extinguisher. The apocalyptic landscape is complete.

War is waste, indeed. Inside an office building near the motor pool.

Quartermaster Avenue

Unidentified equipment room on Quartermaster Avenue. The stairs at the far end of the photograph lead up to the roof.

Mechanical components inside a Quartermaster Avenue compound structure.

Colorful old-time travel trunks inside a quartermaster building.

George S. Patton Jr. NCO Family Housing (The Abandoned City)

The George S. Patton Jr. NCO housing complex is so enormous that I've come to call it "The Abandoned City".

It is hard to see where the rows upon rows of abandoned housing units end.

Well-preserved remains of a children's playground at the housing complex.

Reminders that the George S. Patton Jr. NCO housing complex was once populated by families with children, are still to be found all around the grounds.

Inside the kitchen of a deserted family home.

Charred remains of a family home at the Abandoned City. Fairly easily accessible for a while now, the place attracts vandals, drug addicts and squatters. This damage was the result of a recent fire that was most likely started intentionally by an unidentified individual.

Dawn sets over the ruins of the George S. Patton Jr. NCO housing complex.

AROUND THE BASE

Guard tower at the former Fort Ord brig.

Jaime C. and Jaime A.'s lockers.

Inside a large cafeteria on the Ford Ord campus.

5

TREASURE ISLAND

The Treasure Island of today appears much changed from its unusual beginnings as the staging grounds for the 1939 Golden Gate International Exposition and its later stint as a naval station. The manmade, landfilled island that sits in adjacent contrast to the naturally occurring, jagged rocks of Yerba Buena is one of the stops on the Bay Bridge route spanning the San Francisco Bay. Throughout its lifespan, it has played many roles, and its metamorphosis still continues today.

The island was constructed by the U.S. Army Corps of Engineers and completed on August 24, 1937. Originally intended to reincarnate as a secondary airport for the San Francisco area after the completion of the 1939 Expo, such plans went awry with the quick realization that a much larger plot of land would be needed to accommodate advances in aircraft technology and the growing popularity of international air travel. The proximity to the newly built Bay Bridge, which was already becoming ever busier with vehicular traffic, also posed a safety concern. The idea was scrapped for good when the threat of war became real, and in February 1941 the Navy took over, leasing the island from the city of San Francisco.

Naval Station Treasure Island was known as the gateway to the Pacific during the Second World War. Over four million sailors and soldiers shipped out from the base to destinations all over the Pacific theater of the conflict. A special embarkation camp was even built on the northeastern side of the island in 1944 to more efficiently process the large numbers of troops awaiting departure. The freshly converted naval station provided training that prepared the crews of Navy ships for service on different types of vessels, and also had a large number of WAVES (Women's Appointed Volunteer Emergency Service) personnel operating on site. A myriad of facilities with different functions soon came into existence on the island. Among them were a frontier base for repairing warships, and a naval hospital that opened on April 4, 1942 and treated casualties from the Pacific War until 1947.

Despite the rapid demilitarization and downsizing after World War II's end, it was obvious the Navy was there to stay. Treasure Island remained a naval facility throughout the Cold War, serving once more as an embarkation station, training center and even a supply depot. A Damage Control School, complete with a dedicated wet trainer dubbed USS *Buttercup,* and a firefighting school, were only two of many school divisions that provided technical training courses to naval personnel on the island during this time. Fleet maintenance activity also continued. Military personnel that passed through Treasure Island, either for training or embarkation, participated in operations in the Korea, Vietnam and Persian Gulf conflicts.

Until BRAC interfered in 1991, Treasure Island remained on a military footing, and was off-limits to the civilian population. Then, six years later, when Naval Station Treasure Island's checkpoint booth closed its doors for good, just like that, the once forbidden became accessible to the everyday citizen.

I have been photographing the island since 2008 and I have seen its transformation from a fascinating time capsule of local military history to yet another San Francisco neighborhood in confused transition. Modernization and development are being forced upon the former naval station, often without regard for history and preservation, and the peace that permeated the abandoned space in the first decade or so after closure can no longer be felt there.

Some of the original buildings have burnt down, while others, like the Sage and Cosson Hall twin barracks, have been demolished. The most solid ones of them all, such as the former Pan American Clipper hangars and the administration building, are still around, just living different lives. They are now homes for businesses and sometimes even movie sets (the hangar buildings served as sound stages for *The Matrix* and the administration building with its unique shape substituted for the Berlin Airport in *Indiana Jones and the Last Crusade*). Whatever the future might hold for this unique island, whether it be soccer fields and condos or further decades of decay and oblivion, it will, regardless, remain an iconic local feature, whose exploits and storied past will at the very least live on in photographs.

The uniquely shaped Naval Station Treasure Island administration building is the first thing that the visitor sees upon entering the old base. Its easily accessible location and its Hollywood connection (it stood in for the Berlin Airport in *Indiana Jones and the Last Crusade*) make it an attraction for curious tourists.

The old Naval Station Treasure Island bowling alley at 620 Avenue I.

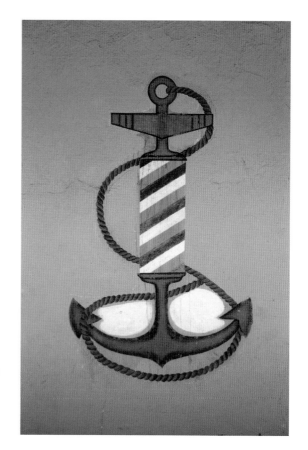

Right: Anchor wall decal on the outside of a Naval Station Treasure Island building.

Below: At the corner of Avenue I and 4th Street.

Time stands still at the Basilone Theater, named after Medal of Honor recipient John Basilone. Movie night comprises of a pair of 1996 releases and a 1988 Disney animated feature.

Graffiti and rust now cover the Olympic-size swimming pool of the former naval base.

The decrepit exterior of a wooden World War II-era building on the island.

A view inside the medical and dental clinic that once functioned on Naval Station Treasure Island.

A view toward the Bay Bridge from the top of one of the steam plant towers, located on the northeastern side of the island.

The remains of Sage Hall—one of two twin barracks buildings (Cosson Hall being the other one) on Treasure Island. The halls had an interesting architectural style—viewed from the air, they each resembled a six-rayed star. Both have since been destroyed to make room for new development on the island.

A frying pan left behind in a barracks room in Cosson Hall. The building no longer stands.

400 AVENUE H

WARNING
RESTRICTED AREA
KEEP OUT

PUBLIC WORKS

IN CASE OF
EMERGENCY

NOTIFY
PWC Code 600
Trouble Desk
302-6171

Decay and a collection of colored signs create a wild variety of textures at 400 Avenue H. The steam plant, also known as Building 455, was once located here.

6

ANGEL ISLAND

It might not be the most famous of the Bay Area islands (such dubious honor must go to that tourist trap, Alcatraz), but persevere past the hordes of schoolchildren on what seems to be a perennial series of field trips, and you might find there is much to love about Angel Island.

The largest natural island in the San Francisco Bay is nowadays a California state park, famous for its immigrant processing station that functioned on site from 1910 until 1940, and popular for its hiking trails and camping sites. Complete with genuine artifacts and original buildings, the immigrant past of Angel Island is interesting and worth exploring at least once, but beyond it lies an even more fascinating world of local military history, including well preserved remains dating back to the Civil War era.

Ever since the island separated from the mainland during the last glacial period about 10,000 years ago, it has occupied a strategic position within the San Francisco Bay. As it often happens throughout history, the U.S. Army was the first to see an opportunity. To guard San Francisco from a Confederate naval attack, artillery batteries were positioned on the island in 1863, setting the foundation for what would later become Camp Reynolds (West Garrison)—a permanent installation on the west side of the island, the remains of which still endure today.

Something had to fill in the other side's shores, and thus the late 1800s saw the building of what is still creatively called the East Garrison, and more formally Fort McDowell. With the government and the armed forces fully moved in, harbingers of the inglorious later uses of the island began to manifest. Partly as a reaction to a bubonic plague scare in the late-nineteenth century, and partly a reflection of the prejudices of the time, a quarantine station was created in 1891, to screen and detain passengers arriving to San Francisco from Asia. Mistreatment and suboptimal conditions were the norm during the station's fifty-plus-year stint. It lasted until 1946, when all its functions were transferred to facilities in San Francisco, with most of its buildings eventually destroyed.

What came later is what most people still come for today—the immigration station and its remains. From 1910 until 1940, when its administration building was destroyed by fire, the station was the first entry point for immigrants, mostly Asian, on their way to San Francisco. During the World War II years, German, Italian and Japanese prisoners of war were also processed through the rehabilitated facilities. The mistreatment that had become the shameful standard during the quarantine station days continued into the era of the immigration station.

It has been a story of arrivals. The Army got there first, the immigrants came after and in 2018, I also arrived at last. Ignorantly, I must confess, I also came for the immigration station, as well as to explore the natural beauty of the place. I quickly found out, however, that it held much more than I had originally anticipated.

The well–preserved nineteenth-century officers' quarters of Camp Reynolds still line the spacious parade ground, and Fort McDowell is a magnificent and photogenic ruin, its buildings scattered on the eastern side of the island. The Camp Reynolds hospital, while decrepit and fairly rotting, presents a grandiose sight when first encountered in all its ghostly glory. And a simple stroll around the hiking paths of the island, even without any goal in particular, seems to reveal small remnants and artifacts of the many incarnations of this enigmatic place.

In the two visits that I have paid so far, I am yet to explore the entirety of the island—this is how large and rich in content it really is. Fortunately, the location's status as a California state park means that some of the historic structures actually appear cared for. In view of this, there might be hope yet for the Isla de los Ángeles (as its discoverer, Juan de Ayala, termed it centuries ago) to endure not only as a memorial to California's immigrant past, present and future, but also as a place that values and preserves the military history, which is also a vital part of its fabric.

Above: The exterior of the Camp Reynolds hospital.

Right: Stairwell leading from the basement to the top floors of the Camp Reynolds hospital.

An early twentieth-century radiator with intricate decorations lies deserted upon the basement floor of the Camp Reynolds hospital.

Room number 332 at the Camp Reynolds hospital.

Right: Ammunition storage in the basement of the Camp Reynolds hospital building. The interior of the structure is fully dark and has to be lit by torch.

Below: Wooden lockers of all sizes are built into the walls of the Camp Reynolds hospital. They were part of the remodel when the building changed hands and purpose in 1923, becoming part of the Quartermaster Corps.

Urinal and sink that look to be from the original build, located in one of the upper floor bathrooms of the Camp Reynolds hospital.

Decay envelops the upper floors of the Camp Reynolds hospital. A period-piece radiator from the early twentieth century can still be seen in its place near one of the windows.

Some of the wooden wall cabinets of the Camp Reynolds hospital that were put in around 1923, when the building was transferred from the Medical to the Quartermaster Corps. The former hospital was converted for office and barracks use after the handoff.

A smaller Civil War-era building that was part of the Camp Reynolds hospital complex.

Interior of officer housing building at Camp Reynolds.

The collapsed facade of the Immigration Station hospital building near Point Simpton.

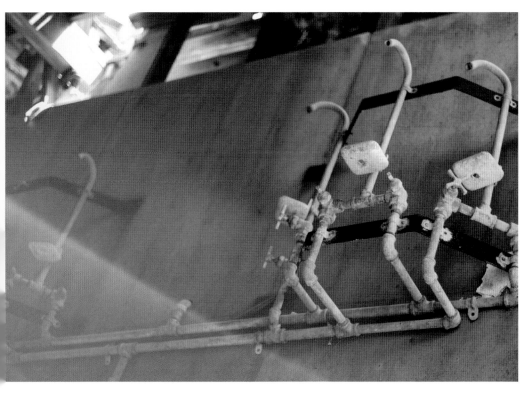

Old shower heads now rust in the ruins of the Immigration Station hospital building.

The interior of the Fort McDowell hospital building. The stairs have been removed to prevent access to the top floors.

In the courtyard of the Fort McDowell hospital. Built in 1911, this massive, new construction building replaced the old Camp Reynolds hospital as the primary care facility on Angel Island.

The exterior of the post exchange building at Fort McDowell (East Garrison).

7

RICHMOND'S GENERAL WAREHOUSE

E ven amidst the enormity of Shipyard Number Three in Richmond, California, it is hard to miss the imposing concrete mass that is the General Warehouse. When I first explored the historic Richmond Shipyards complex in 2015, I did not know the name, the origins or the purpose of the otherworldly-looking building before me, but I immediately became curious when I stumbled upon it in the dark that night. After that first visit, I had to know more about this unique structure.

It turns out that the design for the monolith started out as a rough sketch on the back of an envelope by chief Shipyard Number Three architect, Morris Wortman, as he was returning to California after a visit to Kaiser offices in New York. The General Warehouse was considered the most important structure intended for the third shipyard in the series at the time of its conception. It was built by Cahill Bros. in the Streamline Moderne style (a late variation of Art Deco), with curved corners, horizontal banding and decorative porthole windows. Driven by the urgency of war, the General Warehouse took only 120 days to be completed—another feat of expediency in production that was starting to become the norm at the Richmond Shipyards.

At Shipyard Number Three, the General Warehouse was the last in a series of facilities that were laid out sequentially from north to south, and was a part of the Outfitting zone of operation (the other three being Engineering, Hull Construction and Administration). As the name suggests, buildings in this zone were directly associated with vessel outfitting activities that occurred post-launch. Being the last stop for newly produced ships, the General Warehouse provided them with their final furnishings. Here, the vessels received any material goods and equipment, such as stoves, blankets, wastebaskets, mops and anything else that they would need for full functionality.

It was a few years before I finally returned to the shipyards—this time, to visit the SS *Red Oak Victory* museum—a Victory ship that was a 1944 product of the Richmond Number 1 Yard. Soon enough, I had a run-in with the ubiquitous security guard that is the bane of the explorer, while walking about the outside perimeter of the warehouse building and taking a few photos. Tired of being given the same old lecture about "private property" and "trespassing," I inquired as to the warehouse owner's identity and their whereabouts. I wanted to see if I could actually take some pictures of the structure for documentation purposes, with their permission, and without being hassled.

To make a long story short, owing to the understanding attitude and kind assistance of the Port of Richmond (the owners of the warehouse), I was actually given access to photograph the inside of this unique historic building. I made the most of the opportunity, spending hours taking images inside the dark sarcophagus on a rainy, cold day in January 2018. As the concrete behemoth had been sitting unused for decades, and was deprived almost entirely of electrical power, I spent my time there in near complete darkness. The sounds of dripping water and bird cries were all around while I explored all four floors of the gigantic building, light painting long exposure photographs with my torch. It was an experience I would repeat in a heartbeat.

When I finally emerged into the gray, rainy afternoon that day, many thoughts crowded my mind. Chief among them was the nagging, unanswered question of what will happen to this historic place. Will it survive the changing times around it without an immediate purpose to fulfill, or would this orphan of war become another victim of so-called modernization and ceaseless new construction? In an environment where preservation and reverence for history are often disregarded in favor of overdevelopment, profit and greed without regard for heritage, nothing is guaranteed.

As I sloshed through puddles on the way back to the car, I was struck once more by the imposing exterior of the building I had just departed from. For the first time, I noticed that a portion of the original "General Warehouse" metal sign still remained, maimed and rusted, yet awesome in its display above the entrance at 1324 Canal Boulevard. It was then I was reminded again of how powerful images can be and how important they are to raising awareness about their subjects. In this tale of ghosts of past and present, I believe it is fitting that the images of the General Warehouse building have the last word. It is my hope that it will be a tale that still has a few chapters left.

The imposing exterior of the Richmond General Warehouse at night.

The first floor dispatch office and the skyway above it, connecting two sections of a faux second floor enclosure on top.

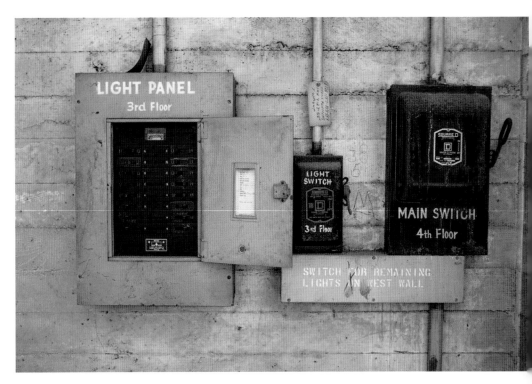

The light panel on the third floor of the warehouse retains its original labels and font and is remarkably intact.

A comfortable looking chair in a remarkably preserved condition sits next to what looks to be one of the break rooms on the second floor. It is located next to an equally intact blue couch.

One of the warehouse's massive freight elevators. Once the workhorses of the operation, they now rust away in the darkness of the giant structure.

One of the freight elevator rooms, located on the warehouse's roof.

One of the loading docks, now perennially closed for business. The dispatch office is on the left.

A lone chair still waits for its occupant to return and continue gazing out the window at the decaying remnants of a once active Shipyard Number Three.

Entering the darkness of floor number two.

Ghostly encounters on floor two of the Richmond Shipyards General Warehouse.

A wooden compartment on the fourth floor, constructed within the concrete shell of the outer building and featuring two levels. Unlike the darkness abounding everywhere else in the warehouse, it was well lit by two fluorescent light fixtures.

One of the signature round windows of the warehouse building—this one located in a men's room. Underneath, an old paper dispenser is being devoured by rust and the passage of time.

A look into the network room on the first floor, with telecommunication patch bays and vintage computer systems on display.

What remains of the old General Warehouse metal sign at 1324 Canal Boulevard.

CONCLUSION

So, in the end, I must ask again—both of myself, and rhetorically—why the San Francisco Bay Area? Why write a book about the neglected and decaying side of this region that some want to forget ever existed? The short answer must be that I want people to know that there was another side to this place before it became the land of ubiquitous tech. There was a land of large-scale industrial production, of naval bases and army life, and in a way, of a more diverse and colorful culture and society. And while the abandoned remains of this previous life are not in themselves indicators of a better environment, they are now the only reminders, such because sturdily built, of a time that no longer exists. Most of the nature and orchards that once covered this area, though not pertinent to this book's subject matter, did not live to tell the tale—they now have buildings growing on top of them. Today, the region where once a more well-rounded and varied landscape and a more natural, balanced way of life was the norm, seems all but gone.

In this book, I have told the tales of but a few of Northern California's abandoned historical sites. For the seven locations described here, there are probably hundreds more that are suffering the same fate, sitting in decay, left behind and uncared for, while the modern era passes them by and erases any trace of their existence.

I have relayed the stories in my own way, in my own words, from the perspective of one who is enamored with these left-behind worlds that most others consider unsightly and unworthy. This is not a traditional photography book or a guide to obscure destinations, and it has not been written as either. For me, the only way to create this work was to tune in to the inspiration I feel from years of visits to these unique places, and to process the energy I receive through my own understanding of what it all means to the bigger picture of things. The desire to share the inspiration I receive from these ugly ducklings of civilization has also been a motivating factor.

Inevitably, living in the Northern California Bay Area for over two decades has also colored my impressions. But I don't think this is wrong, or that it takes anything away from the work. On the contrary, it places this writing in a proper context and hopefully addresses some of the flaws in our local mentality that prevent a more favorable outcome for places of historical and societal value. The good news is that with the right attitudes and effort, perhaps some of this history can still be reintegrated into society for the benefit of all.

In parting, more than a work of description that just entertains, may this be a work of commentary on the bigger human picture and our attitudes toward our cities, our common space, our society and our history—not only in the San Francisco Bay Area, but beyond. The sites described here, and all abandoned destinations from a time before the all-encompassing technological boom, are a part of the region as much as startups, innovation and venture capital. They are a history that we should acknowledge, rather than just view as more real estate space that we can repurpose for future use.

May this also be a work that makes the reader stop and think—about the things we place value on, about where beauty truly lies, and about whether or not our idea of what a diverse and well-rounded society should look like is correct in its current form. And may it be a work that ultimately takes us beyond mere observation of the hidden and forbidden corners of our planet, and into reflection upon the bigger issues they represent, as well as the insight into human nature they mutely, yet powerfully, provide. Because sometimes, it takes a look into the dark corners of life to realize where the well-lit way to future progress truly lies.

All photographs © Manol Z. Manolov
Disclaimer: Trespassing on federal or private property is in no way encouraged or condoned.

ABOUT THE AUTHOR

MANOL Z. MANOLOV is photographer and writer born in Bulgaria and now based in the San Francisco Bay Area. He has a passion for documenting abandoned history and travels the world doing so. Finding beauty where others might not is a creative challenge and a personal interest that continues to drive his efforts behind the camera. You can visit him at www.manolmanolovphotography.com

Author: © by Nikolay Bratovanov, www.nikolaybratovanov.com